To Zoë and to Gabriel,
and to their beautiful babies.

Text, pictures and concept by Patrizia Nobbe
Five Fun and Meaningful Crafts for Kids
Published January 2026 ©
ISBN: 979-8-218-94146-8

www.little-futures.net

AUTHOR'S NOTE

I deeply trust in learning by doing.

There are so many skills I want to teach my daughter, Rhea. I want her to know that we don't just go to a store and buy—we create, we fix, and we design. Making things builds confidence, sparks curiosity, brings joy, and allows one to get wonderfully colorful and messy.

Soon after Rhea was born, I started collecting materials with "art potential" from friends, nature, and even the sidewalk. I wanted to teach her the habit of curiosity: to look at a reusable item and see what it could be, rather than what it was.

Many of these projects were born from necessity or nostalgia: broken or missing pieces, or the games I had created as a child when I couldn't buy them. Each project reflects a different medium and philosophy, but they all show children how ordinary objects—often overlooked or discarded—can be transformed into something valuable and fun.

Creating these projects with Rhea has been a joy. Even when she was very young, I invited her input—like with The Snake Game (p.20). She still sees her influence every time we play it, and we've since built new versions using her evolving painting skills.

You can involve your child in every stage of these five projects, meeting them exactly where they are:

- Collaborate: Decide together which project to tackle and where to find the materials.
- Create: Let them paint, cut, collect, and prepare.
- Explore: Figure out how to construct something together.

The projects are designed to be flexible. Break them into short sessions tailored to the time you have. However you approach them, they will nurture creativity and create lasting memories with your kids.

Table of Contents

How to Use This Book

Keep it simple.
Make it fun.

1. Choose Your Adventure

Start by flipping through the pages together.
Ask your child, *"What do you want to make?"*

Pick just **two** projects to get started:

- **Create a Game** (p. 5-7): Invent your own fun and rules.
- **Natural Ink** (p. 8-11): Turn nature into art supplies.
- **Art Organizer** (p. 12-16): Learn book-binding skills while tidying up.
- **Small Sculptures** (p. 17-20): Replace a missing game piece or make a tiny friend.
- **Hidden Compartment** (p. 21-23): Build a larger object with a secret inside.

2. The Scavenger Hunt

Once you've picked a project, check the **"COLLECT"** tab. Take your time gathering your "trash-to-treasure" supplies—save those tissue papers, paper bags, and food jars!

3. Teamwork by Age

Get the kids involved at their own pace.

The Explorers (Ages 3–4):
- **Hunt:** Find cardboard at home or sticks and acorns in the park.
- **Build:** Help with gluing and handling textures.
- **Art:** Splash on the paint and decorate the big surfaces.

The Designers (Ages 5–6):
- **Create:** Assist with cutting and assembly.
- **Plan:** Help dream up the concept and design the details (like fish scales or game tokens).

Do the projects at your own pace, and when you've done as much as you like, pass it on to the next family of creators!

The Fishing Game

The Fishing Game

Time frame: A weekend afternoon, or take several weeks

COLLECT

- **Cardboard** from packaging
- **Magnets** that can be tied to a string
- Little *magnetic* **metal** items that may be attached to the "fish": paper clips, curtain clips or staples
- **Sticks** e.g. from a park, for fishing rods (ca. 30" | 70cm)
- **String** for each fishing rod (30" | 70cm)
- **Scissors**
- **Stapler** (if you have one)
- Paints, pens, stickers, glitter to decorate
- A "**fish bucket**" (a big bowl?)

Rhea's first fish, with my support. She didn't want to cut it out. Mouth is a metal key ring, attached with a stapler.

The Fishing Game

Remember fishing out of imaginary ponds as a kid, with plastic or cardboard fish with a stick, string and magnets? This version is about making big fish yourselves, standing on a sofa with your fishing rod, getting them off the floor.

Lessons: Planning a long-term project. Exploring magnetism.
Outcome: A game the family can play, and that you can expand.

First, **introduce the idea** of making fish (or, if they are a little older, introduce making a game). Second, **collect** useful **things**: cardboard, paper, sticks, strings, metal objects. Then select, design, cut and assemble.

1. **Make fish** from recycled boxes and cardboard. Trace and cut fish shapes with your child and offer help where needed.

   Optional: Cut out two same shapes, stuff them with paper or light weight packaging material for a 3D fish effect before stapling them together.

2. **Decorate** your fish with paints, stickers or light-weight fabric.

3. Glue, clip, staple or tie **light metal items to fish mouths**, to make the fish magnetic.

4. **Fishing rod**: Tie one end of the string to your stick, and tie a magnet to the other end.

TIPS

Make one or two fish at a time or as you find new materials. At least 10 fish is a good number for the game. Try to use light materials for the fish and match magnet strength to fish weight and metal size: smaller, lighter fish can be lifted simply using staples or paper clips, heavier fish need a bigger metal piece – curtain clips are great for those. (I may or may not have taken one or two curtain rings off our living room curtain.) Key rings I found in the back of a drawer.

Rules of the Game: The Fishing Game

Multiple players take turns catching fish from the floor and carefully lifting them into a bowl or bucket. Different points for different sized fish are an option. However, the kids always win.

Acorn Caps Ink

Acorn Caps Ink

Side Project: Chess "Board"

Hem or cut out a **13"x13" | 33cmx33cm** (or larger) square of **paper** or canvas.

Measure out 8x8 equal sized fields: with a long **ruler** mark 8 evenly sequenced spots vertically and horizontally.

You can carefully freestyle the fields with **a paint brush** and **acorn caps ink**, or use long lines of **tape** to help shape all horizontal lines by taping them off, and then the vertical ones to create fields, and more easily paint within those lines.

Acorn Caps Ink

Time Frame: A weekend afternoon in the fall

COLLECT

- 2–3 handfuls of **acorn caps**
- 5 cups (or 1.2 liters) of **water**
- 2–3 **rusty nails, screws,** or any piece of rusty metal
- 1 **stick** (or old spoon) for stirring
- 1 **old cooking pan**/ pot and sieve
- 1 tiny **screw top vessel** (medicine bottle, or a glass spice jar with lid) to hold the ink
- 1 **funnel** (that fits into the ink vessel)
- 1 **clove**
- 1–3 paper **coffee filters** (cut to funnel size)
- a finger nail sized measure of **Gum Arabic** (or try chick pea liquid instead)

Acorn Caps Ink

FALL PROJECT

Take advantage of fall's acorn bounty to create a rich, dark grey-brown ink. Ink serves numerous purposes: use it as a medium to explore the art of calligraphy and ink drawing, do watercolor experiments by diluting the ink with water and explore layering. I recommend collaborating to craft a roll-up chess board!

Lessons: Use nature. Recognize oaks and acorns. Create ink or paint.
Outcome: Make your own art materials from nature.
Side Project: Use your own natural materials to make a game (see pg. 9).

1. **Collect** a bag of **acorn caps** in the forest, park or in your back yard. Rinse and clean them in an old pot. And collect **rusty screws or nails**, under adult supervision.

2. **In an old cooking pan** *boil* acorns caps with rusty items in five cups/ 1.2 l water (under supervision!) for about two hours. The idea is to reduce the liquid. Check regularly.

3. In the meantime, also **sterilize** a little ink bottle or vessel (by boiling in water) and prepare as shown: a **funnel lined with a coffee filter** – feel free to cut the latter to fit into the designated ink vessel.

Take it off the stove:

4. The ink is **ready** when you can scrape across the bottom of the pan and the dark thickish ink liquid doesn't immediately merge again: just a touch thicker than water. Now *immediately* and *carefully* pour hot liquid through coffee filter-lined funnel into the prepared vessel. Keep acorns from tumbling out of the pot with pot lid. It's important to get the ink out of the hot pot as soon as possible, because it evaporates. Passing the ink through the funnel may take a while - in that case, let sit overnight.

5. **Add 1 clove,** and a tiny bit of **Gum Arabic** (substitute: chick pea liquid) to ink at the end, maybe a third of a tea spoon max. These thicken the ink just a bit, so that it doesn't run off the page.

Use Ink

Use ink on different materials, with fountain pens. Refill old felt tip pens by soaking their sponges in ink overnight; dilute ink for water colors and use with brushes - or go next-level and create a chess board (see pg. 9).

The Art Diary

Time Frame: Two weekend afternoons

COLLECT

- 3 large pieces of **sturdy cardboard** to make the folder: front and back covers (17"x11" | 40cmx28cm) and spine (17"x6" | 40cmx15cm) Make sure the folder can accommodate at least letter-size paper.
- Collect another 3 pieces of **thinner cardboard or just paper** -same sizes as above- for the inner cover (don't buy new paper; glue together different pieces of old paper and cut in shape; these don't have to carry weight and are mainly for show).
- **Paper and tape** to hold everything together, pictured in beige below: large paper (ca. 31"x19" | 78cmx49cm) plus duct tape to fortify. OR use a piece of _fabric_ instead (e.g. old kids pajamas).
- **Strong glue** (borrow a glue gun?), **scissors**, **ruler**.
- **Paints, decorative tape or elastics** to decorate. Feel your way through the project.

1 Assemble three cardboard elements (brown in the pic) and glue them onto one large sheet of strong paper or piece of fabric (beige in the pic). (We'll cut that to size in the next step.) These pieces will form the back, front and spine of your folder, with the paper/ fabric holding it together, so leave gaps between pieces to enable opening and closing.

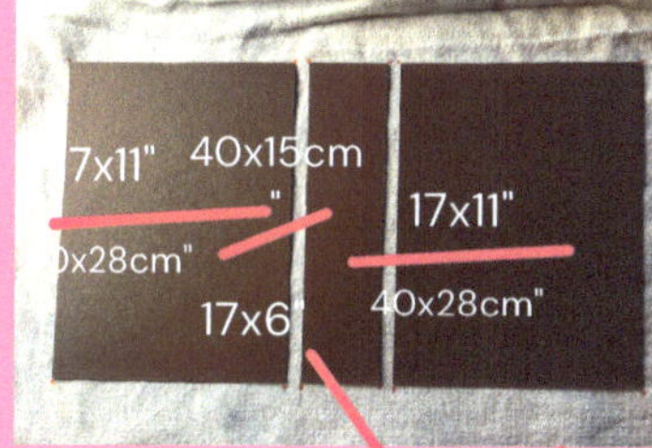

2 Cut that large sheet of paper or fabric as pictured so that you have 0.4" to fold over and glue on the insides of cover, spine and back.

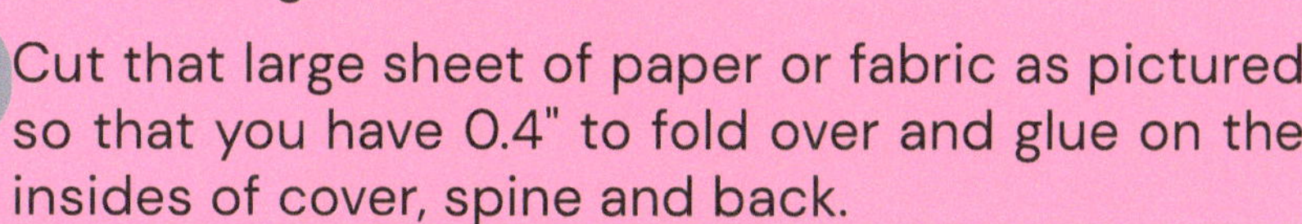

3 Fold and glue the edges of the paper/ fabric base to the inside as shown. If you used paper, use duct tape to fortify especially the creases. If your duct tape does not look pretty, do it on the inside.

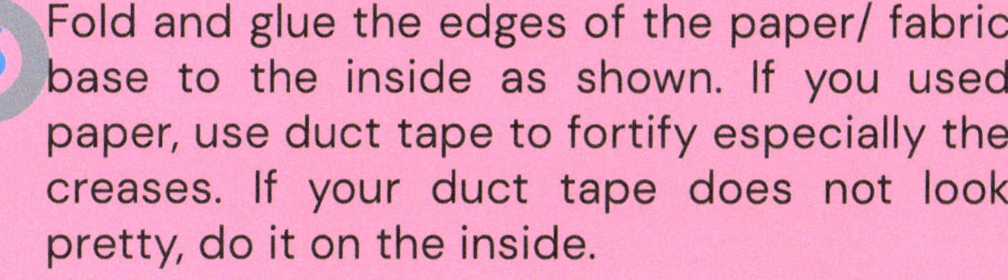

Gap!
Fabric or paper

5 Decorate inside out and enjoy the finished folder.

4 To pretty up the inner cover: Glue the second set of three pieces (here turquoise) on top of their base elements, to hide the glued-over fabric/ paper edges, and potentially the duct tape.

The Art Diary 

Create a magical book that gathers your child's artworks like a treasure chest! Each summer, I created one to organize my daughter's upcoming artistic creations. On page 12 you see the current collection of five books. They go from right to left, with the partially blue one on the left the current one. Mix, match, and have fun—the only goal is to keep those creative pieces safe and together!

Lessons: Design and build a folder, exploring a variety of techniques, based on what you have. It will be different and better each year! Introduces book-making.

Product: A fun way to keep for your growing child's art in one place - no more loose pieces in a pile or drawer!

① BUILD A FOLDER

You want to build a folder that can stand upright, like a book, doesn't break, and kind of closes.

Somehow connect two equal-sized large rectangles of strong cardboard, and a slimmer one functioning as a spine. (See pics and steps on the previous page.)

② DESIGN AND DECOR

Anything goes. To cover up the recycled cardboard inside out, we use old drawings or paint them. We use decorations that are meaningful to us, like old gift wrap, the jackets from old kids' books, fabric of favorite outgrown pajamas, and more. To attach, I used a borrowed glue gun, but you can also use strong glue.

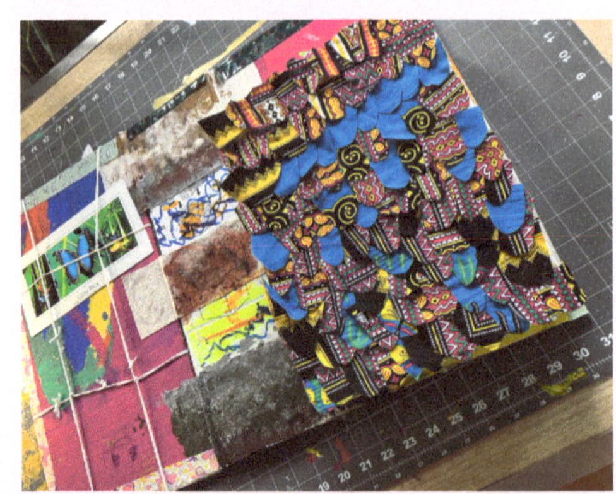

The Art Diary

Three TECHNIQUES to hold art in your folder

1 **Create a pocket**: On the inside of one of the covers, with glue or staples, attach additional cardboard pieces to form a pocket that is open on top, big enough to collect pieces of paper. The goal is to just slide the pieces in and be done.

This year I used an old paper box in the right size and attached it to the inside of the book cover (covered in the blue scales – shown on the lower right picture).

2 **An elastic net**: To hold highly decorative or oddly shaped art pieces, I covered the front with an elastic net. Use flexible string. Stretch two strings vertically and then two horizontally, tying a knot where they meet.

Book-binding: The third technique is a wonderful activity, if, initially, with limited participation by your child. While binding the pages, they can observe how a book of their own artwork is being formed (next page).

③ Book binding:

The first years of art book making, when Rhea was only two and three years old, in a quiet moment I bound her art scribbles in an old-fashioned way. It's tricky for kids to do much at this age but observe. Rhea glued the spines twice.

Arrange the art pages in a neat stack; shake the stack against the table, trying to align the edges to be bound later. That will go a long way towards creating a neat line for the spine.

Then press the stack of art pages *tightly* between **two boards**, using **clamps**, the carefully aligned side upwards (I do it on the floor and stand up the construction for gluing when tight). **Glue** the "spine" glue three times (I used Elmer's), letting it dry 24 hours each time. So, this takes three days and nights.

Then I glued the newly bound pages against the inside of the folder spine, using strong glue.

As Rhea grew older I have stopped binding her art pieces, as they became less predictable and more irregular. At first, I took photos and bound these, but have abandonded "binding" in favor of the easier "pockets".

Game Pieces

Time Frame: One afternoon, or two

COLLECT

- 2 cups (ca. 250g) of all-purpose **flour**
- 3/4 cup (175ml) of **water**
- 1/2 cup (ca. 150g) of (table) **salt**
- A messy-work area **protector**
- A mixing **bowl**
- **Paints** and paint **brushes**

NOTE: This provides quite a bit of dough. If you want to test it or just make a few shapes with a four- or five-year-old, cut the amounts in half.

Game Pieces

Settle down with your little ones and make game pieces to replace any missing parts for board games, create miniatures in any form and color you like, or—for the older kids—turn them into unique jewelry creations!

Lessons: Build 3D objects. Design skills. Develop fine motor skills. Creativity.
Outcome: Game pieces, marbles, replacements for missing parts, and so much more.
Side Project: Introduce a new game design (following page).

A SIMPLE SALT DOUGH

There are a lot of recipes for doughs out there. We like this one, which only uses three ingredients and is very kid-friendly.

1. **Combine flour, water and salt** in a big bowl and mix well.
Knead dough for about **10 minutes** (important!). Then transfer to your work surface and knead more if needed. The finished dough should feel solid, well-integrated, and smooth.

2. Now either form **little shapes**, or roll it out on a floured surface and cut out shapes with cookie cutters.
When you feel you near the end of the shapes (and your patience), preheat oven to 300 degrees°F (150°C)

3. Transfer shapes to ungreased cookie sheets.
Bake for about 30 minutes.
Let shapes cool down!

4. On a work-protected surface, start **painting** the pieces. You can do that immediately, or, better yet, the next day, when the pieces have a chance to dry and harden even more. We have painted pieces with watercolors (in the picture on the opposite page we are using up old watercolor containers), or with acrylics or tempura paints - or possibly even paint sticks - see what you have.

Some recipes recommend spraying with clear polyurethane, but I don't understand its composition so I don't do that.
Rather than eternal durability, the focus here is on the practice of making and design practice, which can be refined over time.

The Snake Game

Hem or cut out a **15"x19" | 38cm x 48cm** (or larger) square of **paper** or **canvas** (I hemmed the latter). Guided by the child's art direction, choose and paint with **paintbrushes** a background color (pink here), let dry. Then first trace (highly recommended), and then paint a long-winding snake in desired colors (here: rainbow). Add playing fields – we stamped 51 ring fields with the bottom of a bottle cap (let dry) and then, the cap facing down, rings around it dipped in gold paint (let dry). Brainstorm designs for two additional elements that animate the game: one sending the player upwards, and one down. We chose golden unicorns for the first, and rain drops for the second. We used acrylic paint for all, on canvas, and gold lacquer that I had around. **Watercolors** on paper work, too! You'll need some **dice**.

Rules of Snake Game

Each player selects their piece and gathers on the snake head. Roll the dice in turn and move your piece the number of fields rolled. If you hit a unicorn hoof, move up to the point of the horn; if you hit the top of a waterfall, slide back down. If you get onto the field of another player, send them back to the puddle of the last waterfall. Goal: To reach the snake tail first (here: a golden sun up top).

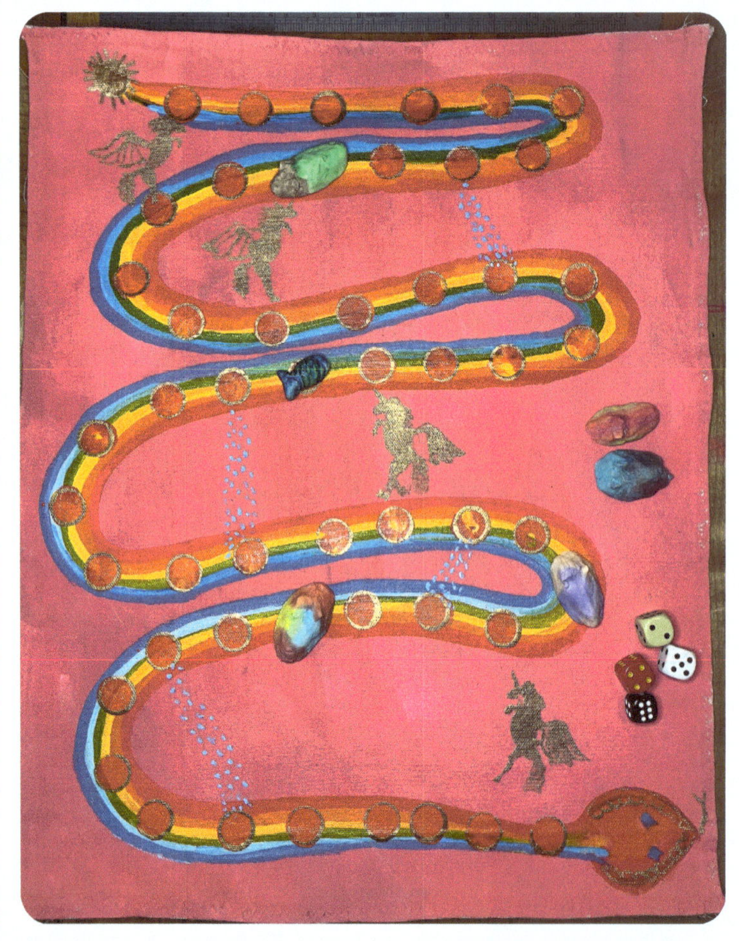

Cat Sculptures

Cat Sculptures HOW TO

Time Frame: One or two weekend afternoons

Foundational shape of Black Cat: Potato chips tube, bottle caps, and scrunched up paper on top for the head. Cover all with 2-4 layers of paper scraps dripping with glue-water mix.

COLLECT

- **Paper scraps**: soft tissue paper, newspaper, expired school info sheets
- **1 shape-providing vessel**: potato chips tube (like Pringles), or a plastic bottle with wide mouth, glass jars – anything with a lid or screw top works.
- Potentially **2-4 bottle caps** or light weight items to give shape to head or legs
- **Paper glue** (I had YES-Paste left), watered down by combining with a little amount of water, so that it is more like a sauce and less like a paste.
- An old saucer, small **bowl** or recycled container for mixing glue/water.
- A **stick** for stirring glue and water.
- A bit of **cardboard** for ears.
- Some **paint** or acorn ink (we used water colors and black and purple acrylics)
- Old **paint brush(es)**

Recycled lid for mixing small amounts of glue/ water

First layer of glue-paper

Potato chips tube: *place upside-down*

Cat Sculptures

This will be messy at first. Tear paper intended for recycling into small pieces and enjoy making charming paper cats—or dogs—with a secret hiding place!

Lessons: Sculptural design, use materials you'd otherwise throw away, rip things apart, get dirty, build 3D objects.

Outcome: A sculpture with a secret hiding place for little treasures.

1. Cover your work area. Rip paper into small pieces (tissue paper, letters, toilet paper wrapping) – rip stronger paper into smaller pieces. Mix a little glue in a bowl with water, stir thoroughly. Set up your screw-top vessel – the foundation for the cat - upside down. Here I describe the making of the Black Cat.

2. Start dipping paper scraps in the glue solution and stick to the upside-down potato chips tube.

Use the Cat

Keep cats open and closable at the bottom and use them to hide secret treasures.

3. Make sure there's 2-4 solid layers of paper covering everything, except the bottom of the container; here leave a small margin to be able to pop the lid back on. Smooth out the paper layers as you go along. We used different recycled items to shape the cat's torso (see opposite pic as well), including bottle caps: glue them to the body and cover with glue-paper scraps. Cut the ear shapes from cardboard and glue on. It's fine to do this in different sessions, drying the cat sculpture as you go and continue molding it later. Mold your cat by adding more paper in some areas, less in others.

4. Once you achieve the desired shape, dry thoroughly and paint - and dry again. We painted the Black Cat with acrylics.
For different cat shapes you can either follow the shape of your vessel or work off a nice image. I formed the Lying Cat pictured on page 21 around bunched up paper. It looked ridiculous at first, then great with watercolors.